Yes, you *can* believe it. The *real* German no teacher dared utter is now on the tip of your tongue:

DAS IST MIR WURST!
(I don't give a flying fig!)

KAPITALISTENSCHWEIN!
(Capitalist pig!)

DER HAT NICHT ALLE TASSEN
IM SCHRANK!
(He's missing his marbles!)

HALT DIE KLAPPE!
(Shut up!)

MACH'NE FLIEGEL!
(Take a hike!)

And dozens more of the lowest German words, phrases, and mini-conversations certain to outrage.

SCHEISSE!
The REAL German You Were Never Taught in School

Gertrude Besserwisser

Illustrated by David Levine

A PLUME BOOK

PLUME
Published by the Penguin Group
Penguin Books USA Inc., 375 Hudson Street,
New York, New York 10014, U.S.A.
Penguin Books Ltd, 27 Wrights Lane,
London W8 5TZ, England
Penguin Books Australia Ltd, Ringwood,
Victoria, Australia
Penguin Books Canada Ltd, 10 Alcorn Avenue,
Toronto, Ontario, Canada M4V 3B2
Penguin Books (N.Z.) Ltd, 182–190 Wairau Road,
Auckland 10, New Zealand

Penguin Books Ltd, Registered Offices:
Harmondsworth, Middlesex, England

First published by Plume, an imprint of Dutton Signet, a division of
Penguin Books USA Inc.

First Printing, July, 1994
40 39 38 37 36 35

 REGISTERED TRADEMARK—MARCA REGISTRADA

LIBRARY OF CONGRESS CATALOGING-IN-PUBLICATION DATA:
Besserwisser, Gertrude.
    Scheisse! : the real German you were never taught in school /
Gertrude Besserwisser : illustrated by David Levine.
        p.   cm.
    "A Plume book."
    ISBN 0-452-27221-1
    1. German language—Slang. 2. German language—Obscene words. 3. German
language—Conversation and phrase books—English.
I. Title.
PF3961.B47   1994
437'.09—dc20   93–48608
                                                                          CIP

Printed in the United States of America
Set in Janson
Designed by Leonard Telesca

BOOKS ARE AVAILABLE AT QUANTITY DISCOUNTS WHEN USED TO PROMOTE PRODUCTS OR
SERVICES. FOR INFORMATION PLEASE WRITE TO PREMIUM MARKETING DIVISION, PENGUIN
BOOKS USA INC., 375 HUDSON STREET, NEW YORK, NEW YORK 10014.

Contents

Preface

So—you spent several valuable years of your youth learning German from *Frau Schultz*, or whatever your teacher's name was, and you conjugated more verbs and declined more articles than you care to remember. And despite those moments of pure torture, you emerged from the entire experience with a feeling of confidence—you think you have a fairly good command of German. Sure. But think again. Aren't there words and expressions *die gute Frau Schultz* never taught you, such as anything relating to, God forbid, *sex*? How about those curses and profanities you take for granted in English but can't find in your dictionary? Most likely, *Frau Schultz* taught you proper High German, and that's fine, of course, as long as you are only speaking to people who have learned German from a textbook. But let's face it, once you are in Berlin or Frankfurt, you will encounter a German rich in idioms and slang, spiced with all sorts of profanities that will leave you flabbergasted or, as the Germans put it, *da wirst du mit den Ohren schlackern* (your ears will be flapping). Wouldn't it be great to understand the natives or be able to impress them with your command of curses and sweet talk? After all, not all your conversations will be held in boardrooms. Hopefully some will take place in bars and bedrooms.

Here, then, is a book that will introduce you to the fine art of cursing, the delicate use of profanities, and some good basic slang to help you navigate the world of spoken German. So when a drunk harasses you in a Frankfurt bar, you'll know just how to tell him to "get lost" or "fuck off" (whichever you prefer); when a woman speaks to you of her *Muschi*, you'll know that she is either talking about her cat or a part of her own anatomy (you be the judge); and when the hitchhiker you picked up on the autobahn yells, *Vorsicht! Bullen!*, you'll know he is not warning you of cattle crossing the road but of the police. While this book can't possibly teach you all there is to know about the creative use of German slang and profanities, it will add some colorful gems to your vocabulary, and who knows, perhaps you will even become a collector of sorts. So for now, don't worry about declinations (if you confuse *mir* and *mich* you're in good company, most Berliners confuse them, too). Just relax and read, and you'll pick up some of the *real* German you were never taught in school.

A Note on Dialects

As you may already know, German is rich in regional dialects. Not only does Austrian German differ from Swiss German, which in turn differs from the German spoken in Germany, but within each of these countries various dialects are spoken. This book is primarily concerned with the German spoken in Germany, and whenever possible dialectic origins of a slang term have been indicated. However, even if a word originated in a certain dialect (say, a Bavarian dialect or a Northern dialect), you can assume that the words included in this book have to some extent crossed dialectic borders. Modern communication being what it is, dialects have begun to mingle and cross-fertilize. For example, the typically Northern German *Tschüß* (informal for "good-bye") has invaded the speech of even the most Southern speakers.

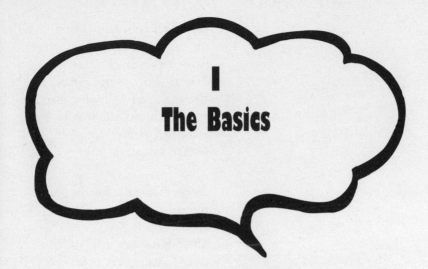

I
The Basics

There are probably few words in *Hochdeutsch* (High German, or proper German) that do not have a more colloquial counterpart. Like English, the German language is alive and well and thrives on a wealth of slang. For starters, here are a few basic colloquialisms and slang that will help you get through your days and nights in Germany. (To refresh your memory, the proper terms precede the profane.)

Folks

man

der Mann
der Kerl (guy; not usually complimentary, but the following combinations are: *guter Kerl*—good guy; *ganzer Kerl*—real man)
der Macker (dude, but also joker)

der Typ (guy, but also character—as in, That character over there)
Heini (bozo; lends itself to the creation of many disparaging compound words; for example, *Sabbelheini*—an overly talkative guy)

old man

älterer Herr (elderly gentleman)
Opa (Grandpa)
alter Knacker (old fart)
der Tattergreis (old geezer)

boy

der Junge
der Knabe (proper but somewhat archaic)
der Bube (Southern variation)
der Buttje (Northern for little boy)
der Bengel (rascal)
der Bursche (youth, guy)

woman

die Frau
das Weib (archaic; however, the plural is still commonly used sarcastically; for example, an exasperated male might exclaim **Weiber!** when his understanding of the other sex reaches its limit)
die Tussi (broad)

2

SCHEISSE!

GANZ KLAR:
DIE ALTE

DIE TUSSI

DAS FLITTCHEN
ODER SOGAR EINE
NUTTE

die **Braut** (literally, bride or bride-to-be, but as slang it means "broad" or "chick")
die **Mutter** (*tolle Mutter*—hot mama or great mom, depending on the context)
das **Flittchen** (tramp)

old woman

ältere Dame (old lady)
Oma (granny)
alte Schachtel (old bag; literally, old box)
die **Fregatte** (a heavily made-up old woman; literally, a frigate)

alte Hexe (old witch)

girl

das Mädchen
das Mädel (connotations range from neutral to endearing, depending on the context)

die Dirn (distinctly Northern; watch out though, add-
ing a final *e* turns it into
Dirne—harlot)
die Schickse (from the Yiddish term for non-Jewess,
but the meaning is a bit
different—it's just as dismis-
sive but can apply to any girl
or young woman)
das Törtchen (literally, tart
but used in a patronizingly
positive sense, as in sweet little thing)
das junge Ding (literally, the
young thing)

friend

der Freund/die Freundin
der Kumpel (buddy)

girlfriend

die Freundin (this is simply
the word for female friend,
just what exactly that means
depends on the context)
die Braut (as explained
above, this term literally
means "bride" but can also
mean "broad," and as such
serves as a lower-class expression for girlfriend)
die Tussi (broad, chick; usually used to deride someone's
girlfriend, so be careful who
you are talking to)

5

boyfriend	**der Freund** (male friend; again, just what that means depends on the context) **der Macker** (any dude, but can also refer to someone's boyfriend; for example, *Ihr Macker hat von nichts eine Ahnung*—Her man is totally out to lunch)
husband	**der Mann** (also means "man") **der Ehemann** (a bit officious) **der Gatte** (old-fashioned but proper) **der Göttergatte** (is used to make fun of one's husband by sarcastically valorizing him) **der Alte** (literally, the old one; a disgruntled wife might refer to her husband as *mein Alter*)
wife	**die Frau** (also means "woman") **die Ehefrau** (officious) **die Gattin** (old-fashioned but proper) **die Alte** (the equivalent of *der Alte*, only, of course, a man would refer to his wife as *meine Alte*)

child	**das Kind** **das Gör** (brat or kid, depending on the context) **der Balg** (brat; applies only to small children)
family	**die Familie** **der Klan** (clan) **der Anhang** (literally, appendage; also entourage, hangers-on, fan club) **die Sippe/Sippschaft** (tribe—fairly derogatory) **Kind und Kegel** (literally, child and bowling pin—implying encumbrance)

Er kam mit Kind und Kegel zum Betriebsausflug.
He brought his entire family (including his mother-in-law and his dog) to the company picnic.

dog	**der Hund** **der Köter** (mutt; beware, Germans are pretty serious about their rottweilers and German shepherds—insulting a man's dog can be a more serious offense than insulting his wife) **die Töle** (mutt) **der Mops** (fat little lapdog) **Fiffi** (fido)

Everyday Necessities

Now that you know what to call folks (including the family dog), consider some of the bare necessities of your German *Alltag* (everyday life)—dough, the john, cops, etc. Yes, cops, not that you will be needing them, but it might be good to know what they are called, just in case.

money	**das Geld**
	die Knete (dough)
	die Kohle (literally, coals)
	die Piepen
	die Mäuse (literally, mice)
	die Moneten
	der Zaster (dough)
	eine Stange Geld (literally, a stick of money—meaning a lot of money)
to pay	**zahlen**
	löhnen (to fork over)
	blechen (to shell out)
	ausspucken (to cough up)
	abdrücken (literally, to squeeze off)
	rüberrücken (to come across with money)
to bribe	**bestechen**
	schmieren (to grease someone's palm)

Considering that Germans build some fine cars, it may not be surprising that they spend a lot of time puttering on them. But you may be amazed at how serious they are about these little heaps of metal (plastic) and rubber. Unlike a Frenchman who could care less how many dents his car has, a German is likely to throw a fit if you just so much as gently tap his car. And because Germans are very particular about their cars, they have a lot of words for them. Here are just a few.

car

das Auto/der Wagen
die Kiste (literally, box— fairly neutral)
der fahrbare Untersatz (set of wheels; for example, you might ask, *Hast du einen fahrbaren Untersatz?*—Do you have a set of wheels?)
der Schlitten (literally, sled—complimentary term; *toller Schlitten* means "great car," especially "a great looking car")
der Amischlitten (*Ami* means "American," but not just any American car— imagine a long, sleek Cadillac)
der Flitzer (fast car)
die Schese (old clunker)
die Nuckelpinne (old clunker that surprisingly still moves, even if only at a snail's pace)
die Rostlaube (only the rust still holds it together)
die Zitrone (lemon—both the car and the fruit)

SCHEISSE!

A car you will see a lot in East Germany is a *Trabbi*, short for *Trabant*, a genuine product of the GDR. You may want to keep your windows closed in the wake of a *Trabbi:* it has a two stroke engine and leaves an incredible blue cloud of exhaust.

motorcycle	**das Motorrad** **der heiße Ofen** (literally, hot oven) **der Bock** (literally, buck or male deer)
to drive	**fahren** **rasen** (to race; to speed) **brettern** or **heizen** (same as above but more colloquial) **herumfahren** (to cruise)
bicycle	**das Fahrrad** **der Drahtesel** (literally, wire donkey)

Bicycles are almost as popular in Germany as cars, and while bicyclists are less neurotic than drivers, they can, nonetheless, be equally aggressive. Make sure you don't park your car on a bike path (that black or red little strip between the sidewalk and the road), or some irate bicyclist may slash your tires.

thing	**das Ding** **die Sache** (for example, *Ich habe eine dumme Sache gemacht*—I've done a stupid thing)

11

das Teil (literally, piece; wildly used among young people to refer to just about any object; for example, *Das ist ein super Teil*—That's a cool piece—could refer to a pair of jeans, a CD player, a car, anything; the objective here is to sound cool)
das Dingsda (when you can't think of the name of a thing)

While we're talking about **Dingsda:**

what's-his-name	**der Dingsda**
what's-her-name	**die Dingsda**
garbage	**der Abfall** **der Müll** (trash) **der Dreck** (muck) **der Schrott** (junk; as in *Schrottplatz*—junkyard) **der Ramsch** (junk; as in a cheap and poorly made product)
clothes	**die Kleidung** **die Klamotten** (especially *tolle Klamotten*—cool clothes) **die Plünden** (junk; old clothes)
toilet	**die Toilette** (plain and straight; don't be shy, this is

SCHEISSE!

the word Germans use when they ask for a rest room)
das To (abbreviation of the above, but don't ask me why the article changes)
das WC
das Klo (john, loo)
das stille Örtchen (literally, the small quiet place)
Wo der Kaiser von China allein hingeht (Where the emperor of China goes by himself)

bed

das Bett
die Koje (originally a berth on a ship, but as slang refers to any bed)
die Heia (*in die Heia gehen*—to go to bed)

to sleep

schlafen
pennen
pofen
knacken (deepest variety)

TV

der Fernseher
die Röhre (tube)
die Glotze (from the verb *glotzen*—to stare)
der Flimmerkasten (literally, the glimmer box)

movie theater

das Filmtheater
das Kino (for example, at the movies would be *im Kino*)

music	**die Musik** **die Mukke** (used by musicians; *Laß uns mal zusammen Mukke machen*—Let's make some music together) **das Gedudel** (not a very appreciative term) **der Sound**
newspaper	**die Zeitung** **das Revolverblatt** (tabloid paper, namely *Die Bild-Zeitung*, which happens to be the most widely read newspaper in Germany) **das Käseblatt** (rag; provincial paper not really worth reading unless you want to know which of farmer Schröder's cows died of colic last night)
police	**die Polizei** (also known as **Dein Freund und Helfer**—Your friend and aid) **die Polente** **die Bullen** (literally, the bulls) **das Rindfleisch** (Southern variation; literally, beef)
police car	**der Polizeiwagen** **der Peterwagen** (Pete's car; distinctly Northern)

SCHEISSE!

jail	**das Gefängnis** **der Knast** **das Kittchen** (not to be con- fused with "kitchen")
jailbird	**der Knasti** **der Knastler** **der Knastbruder**
ambulance	**der Krankenwagen** **der Frischfleischwagen** (fresh meat delivery van)

Prima Adjectives

Now that you have some basic slang under your belt, here are a couple of adjectives that will come in handy.

The many ways of saying great or cool:

klasse
super
prima
spitze
toll
geil (watch out, can also mean horny)
affengeil (more emphatic variant of the above, but I have no idea how *Affen*—apes—got involved)
riesig (literally, gigantic)
elefantös (turn elephant into an adjective and you have *elefantös*)

15

For example:

Das ist ja ein geiler Schlitten.
That's a cool car.

Er ist ein toller Kerl.
He's a great guy.

Was? Du hast im Lotto gewonnen? Das ist ja elefantös.
What? You won the lottery? That's great/enormous/wonderful.

But if you want to express your outright disgust, try these:

SCHEISSE!

beschissen (shitty)
mies (rotten, lousy)
lausig (lousy)
ätzend (awful; literally, corrosive)
gemein (mean, but also common, ordinary)
fies (nasty, mean; bordering on sadistic)
blöd (stupid)
doof (dumb)
bescheuert (stupid and ridiculous)

Mir geht es ziemlich beschissen heute.
I'm feeling pretty shitty today.

Diese blöde Tussi ist in mich reingefahren.
This stupid broad drove into my car.

Der Typ da drüben ist ganz schon fies.
That guy over there is a pretty mean character.

If you want to add more emphasis to an adjective, precede it with **total** or **völlig** (respectively, totally and completely). As in, *Der Typ ist völlig bescheuert* or *Das Auto ist total super.* Just try not to call everything and everyone *total super*; it wears out pretty quickly.

Finally, one more basic term that could literally save your life. As you can imagine, knowing all the dialectic variations of the word *no* can turn out to be a vital skill. This is especially true since the Bavarian pronunciation of *no* can cause a bit of confusion. See why:

No

Nein
Ne (Northern)
Nö
Na (Bavarian; however, the
same word means both "Hi"
and "Hey" in High German)

Mini-Monologue

Okay, It's Time to Tune and Test-run
Your Slang

1. Gestern bin ich mit meinem Kumpel in seinem neuen Schlitten durch die Gegend gefahren.
2. Da hielt uns eine Tussi an und fragte, ob wir sie ein Stück mitnehmen.
3. Klar doch, haben wir gesagt. Aber dann kamen noch zwei Typen aus dem Gebüsch.
4. Die sahen total fies aus. Da sind wir lieber weitergefahren.
5. Heute habe ich in unserem Käseblatt gelesen, daß drei Anhalter Heiner Behrens überfallen haben und mit seiner alten Schese abgehauen sind.
6. Die sind aber nicht weit gekommen. Kaum zu glauben, aber die Bullen haben sie geschnappt.

1. Yesterday, my buddy and I were taking his new car for a spin.
2. There was a broad who stopped us and asked if we could give her a ride.
3. Sure, we said. But then two guys came out of the bushes.
4. They looked pretty mean. So we figured, we'd better drive on.

SCHEISSE!

5. Today, I read in our local rag that three hitchhikers robbed Heiner Behrens and took off in his old clunker.
6. They didn't get very far though. Hard to believe, but the cops caught them.

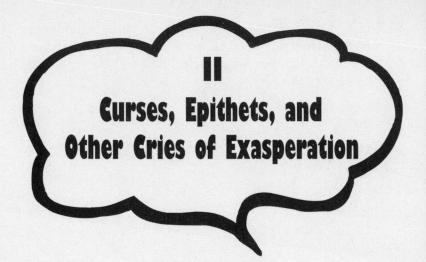

II
Curses, Epithets, and Other Cries of Exasperation

What would your English be without a decent repertoire of curses? Pretty plain. Well, the same is true of your German. Not only do curses add some spice and flavor to our language, but let's face it, they also allow us to communicate pretty effectively. Fortunately, German is a language brimming with curses. And in case you have any reservations about using them, be assured that even classic German literature supplies some earthy vulgarisms. It was Goethe's Götz von Berlichen, after all, who popularized *Du kannst mich mal am Arsch lecken* (You can lick my ass).

Classic German Curses

damn

verdammt
Verdammt noch mal! (literally, damned again; similar to Goddamn it!)
Verdammt und zugenäht! (literally, damned and stitched

tight; smply a more verbose
version of the above)
verflucht (literally, cursed)
Verflucht noch mal!

idiot

der Idiot (for example, *Du
Idiot!* or better *Du
verdammter Idiot*)
der Holzkopf (bonehead;
literally, wood-head)
der Torfkopp (Northern
variation of the above; literally, peat-head)
der Dummkopf (numbskull)
der Trottel (half-wit)

| | der **Armleuchter** (dimwit; literally, candelabra) |
| clumsy person | der **Töffel** (the adjective **töffelig** means "clumsy") der **Tollpatsch** (truly a klutz) |

Er ist so ein verdammter Tollpatsch, er kann nicht einmal eine Glühbirne wechseln ohne sich ein Bein zubrechen.
He's such a damn klutz, he can't even change a light bulb without breaking a leg.

slowpoke	der **Lahmarsch** (literally, lame ass)
asshole	das **Arschloch** der **Arsch** (simply ass, but has about the same effect as calling someone an *Arschloch*) **ein Arsch mit Ohren** (literally, an ass with ears; may sound less vulgar but is pretty insulting)
shithead	der **Scheißkerl**

When things aren't going well, try some of these phrases and expressions:

Ach!
Oh! (an absolutely vital expression, no German can do without it; depending on tonality, you can modulate the meaning from a surprised "Oh!" to a skeptical "Oh, really?" to a completely frustrated "Oh, shit!")

SCHEISSE!

Ach du Scheiße!/Ach du meine Scheiße!
Oh, shit! (more on *Scheiße* later)

Ach du grüne Neune!
Oh, shoot! (*grüne Neune* means green nine; it's simply a way of avoiding "shit")

Mensch!
Man! (another absolutely essential expression; used in response to both pleasant and rude surprises)

Menschenskind!
(literally, child of man; more emphatic variation of the above; for best effect, put a strong stress on the first syllable)

Quatsch!
Baloney!

And when you are about to explode with anger:

Himmel, Arsch und Zwirn!
Goddamn it! (literally, Heaven, ass, and yarn!; a play on the more blasphemous **Himmel, Herrgott, Sakrament!**—Heaven, God, and sacrament)

When you want to give someone the finger:

Du kannst mich mal am Arsch lecken!
Go fuck yourself! (literally, You can lick my ass!; you can also simply say, *Du kannst mich mal!*—and the message will be the same; and if you want to return a salutation of this kind, simply respond with *Du mich auch!*)

23

Geh zum Teufel!
Go to hell! (literally, Go to the devil!)

Or when you think you are being had:

Du willst mich wohl auf den Arm nehmen.
You're trying to pull my leg.

Du willst mich wohl verarschen.
(more vulgar version of the above)

Calling on higher powers:

Jesus Maria!
Jesus Christ! (interestingly, mostly used in the Catholic
South; Protestant Northerners prefer **Du meine Güte!—**
Mercy!; Oh, my goodness; Good gracious)

Um Gottes Willen!
For God's sake!

Oh Gott!
Oh my God!

If you couldn't care less, try these:

Na und?
So what?

Das ist mir scheißegal!
I don't give a shit!

And when you have trouble believing your eyes:

SCHEISSE!

Ich dacht' mich tritt ein Pferd!
I thought I was dreaming! (literally, I thought a horse was kicking me; mostly used when you're telling a story)

Questions of Sanity

Bist du verrückt?
Are you crazy?

Hast du 'ne Meise?
Are you nuts? (literally, Do you have a titmouse?—a titmouse is a small bird)

Or a bit more vulgar:
Sag mal, hast du den Arsch offen?
(loosely, Say, is your ass open or what?)

Der hat nicht alle Tassen im Schrank!
He's missing a few marbles! (literally, He doesn't have all his cups in his cabinet)

While we're at it, a few more words on sanity:

crazy

verrückt
wahnsinnig (insane; also slang for cool or great)
bekloppt (been hit on the head a bit too often; literally, hammered)
nicht ganz dicht (literally, not quite tight—that is, Your brain must be leaking)

meschugge (meshuga, meshuganna)
einen Vogel haben (loony; literally, to have a bird)
eine Schraube locker haben (to have a screw loose)

Privacy via Profanities

If you value your privacy, you have probably discovered that the polite ways of telling someone to leave you alone are not always the most effective ones. So if a drunk is pestering you, or a *Grabbelheini* is molesting you, you might want to consider some stronger medicine.

Laß mich in Ruhe!
Leave me alone!

Mach mich nicht an!
Don't mess with me!

Verzieh dich!
Get lost! (literally, Pull out of here)

Mach'ne Fliege!
Take a hike! (literally, Do as a fly does—that is, fly off)

Verpiß dich!)
Fuck off! (literally, Piss yourself away)

Finally, some epithets that will equip you for the battle of the sexes:

What to Call Women

die dumme Kuh (stupid cow)
die Zimtzicke (a bitchy and quarrelsome woman)
das Luder (a mischievous and sly woman)
die Schlampe (slut)
die Wuchtbrumme (a hefty woman; you'd become claustrophobic if caught in an elevator with her)
die Emanze (short for emancipated woman; some men actually try to use this as an insult and some women perceive it as such—the logic is similar to that of calling someone a liberal in the U.S.)
die linke Titte (literally, leftist tit; obviously quite vulgar—meant to insult women on the left of the political spectrum; but since *link* also means "sinister," the term can also take on a different meaning)

What to Call Men

der hirnlose Ochse (literally, brainless ox; male counterpart to *dumme Kuh*)
der Hund (dog)
das Schwein (pig)
der Schweinehund (bastard; combination of the above—a fine example of German compound nouns)
der Kotzbrocken (basically an asshole; literally, a bit or piece of vomit)
der Fettsack (fatso—the guy has more than a beer belly)
der Freßsack (put a lock on your refrigerator—he eats anything in reach)
der Chaot (he likes to cause turmoil and chaos)

der Chauvi (short for *Chauvinist*; what an *Emanze* would call a man who thinks he can insult her by calling her an *Emanze*)

der Spanner (voyeur, Peeping Tom; but also an expression hurled at lascivious old men even if they are not actually peeping; for example, *Du alter Spanner!*)

EIN ALTER SPANNER VOR DEM FLIMMERKASTEN

Mini-Monologue

Try Out Some of These Curses and Mutterings

1. Himmel, Arsch und Zwirn! Nun ist mir der Auspuff zum dritten mal abgefallen.
2. Dieser verdammte Mechaniker ist so ein Armleuchter.
3. Jesus Maria! Wenn ich den Kerl zufassen kriege. . . .
4. Dieser alte Spanner glotz den ganzen Tag die Tussi an der Rezeption an, statt mal zu arbeiten.
5. Ach du Scheiße! Und jetzt noch eine Stunde im Stau sitzen. Toller Tag!
6. Hat der 'ne Meise? Der Typ will hier tatsächlich Rosen auf der Autobahn verkaufen.
7. Heh, mach 'ne Fliege! Ich kaufe nichts.

1. Goddamn it! Now I've dropped my muffler for the third time.
2. This damn mechanic is such a dimwit.
3. Jesus Christ! If I get hold of that guy. . . .
4. The old voyeur spends all day staring at the receptionist instead of doing some work.
5. Oh, shit! And now I'm gonna sit in a traffic jam for an hour. What a day!
6. Is this guy nuts? He's actually trying to sell roses on the autobahn.
7. Hey, take a hike! I'm not buying anything.

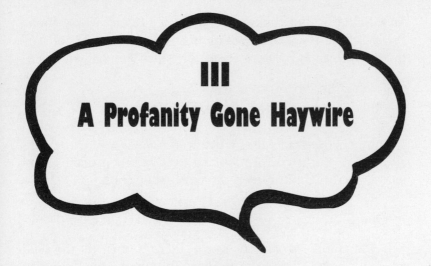

III
A Profanity Gone Haywire

Scheiße

Now let's consider the most commonly used profanity in German, or any other language for that matter. Yes, I'm referring to *Scheiße*, an amazingly versatile word which lends itself to an array of other profane expressions. There is, of course, the garden variety *Scheiße*, a word you have already encountered, but do you know all of its cultivated offspring?

| shit | **die Scheiße/der Scheiß** (use it judiciously; if used in the wrong place it may still raise quite a few eyebrows) **die Schiete/der Schiet** (a less offensive alternative to *Scheiße;* from the Low German dialect still spoken in Northern Germany) |

While **So eine Scheiße** would translate into "Oh, shit,"

So'n Schiet is more akin to "Oh, shoot." (Don't worry about the fact that there are masculine and feminine versions of these two terms. It's doesn't matter which gender you use.)

Other *Scheißwörter*

Another low-grade alternative to *Scheiße* is *der Mist* (literally, dung). But if you are looking for a highly profane alternative, you might consider *die Kacke* (shit, crap).

shitty   **beschissen**

If you think it's a shitty world, then German is the language for you—a language so adept at dealing with the fouler aspects of life that it offers an ingenious alternative to the adjective shitty. Here's what I mean: instead of saying *beschissenes Wetter* for shitty weather, you can say **Scheißwetter.** In fact, you can construct all sorts of compound words with *Scheiße*, such as **Scheißkerl** (shithead), **Scheißauto,** etc. And this compounding works not only for nouns but for adjectives as well. For example, if you want to say "It's fucking cold," you can say **Es ist scheißkalt.** Or if you are completely indifferent about something, instead of saying **Das ist mir egal,** you can say **Das ist mir scheißegal** (as in, I don't give a shit).

Some more offspring of *Scheiße* (keep in mind that they are all vulgar):

der Scheißer (a rotten, shitty person)
der Schieter (while it may sound crude, it's actually used as a term of endearment between husband and wife or among family members)
bescheißen (to screw someone—as in, to trick or cheat someone)

anscheißen (to reprimand severely and rudely; not to confuse you, but sometimes *anscheißen* can also take on the meaning of *bescheißen*)

verscheißern (to pull someone's leg)

der Schiß (originally also shit, but now means mostly "fear"; *Schiß haben*—to have cold feet; to be chicken)

der Beschiß (an act of fraud or cheating)

der Anschiß (a major reprimand from a high-ranking authority figure, as in the military or school)

der Dünnschiß (the runs, diarrhea)

verschissen (to have fucked up, especially to have lost all respect in the eyes of someone else; for example, *Du hast bei mir verschissen* means "You fucked up and I'm through with you")

scheißfreundlich (friendly, but in a phony and saccharin way)

As you can see, *Scheiße* is a fairly flexible word, so try to use it creatively. And to introduce you to a few more applications, here are some choice phrases:

Ach du heilige Scheiße!
Holy shit!

Mach keinen Scheiß!
Don't do anything stupid! (can also mean "Don't kid around with me, this is too serious")

Das geht dich einen absoluten Scheißdreck an.
That is none of your fucking business. (careful, there are hardly any stronger words for such an occasion in German)

Ihm steht die Scheiße bis zum Hals.
He's in deep shit. (literally, He is in shit up to his neck)

SCHEISSE!

Scheiß drauf!
Forget it! (literally, shit on it)

And finally, a pretty verbose saying that doesn't translate well but is well worth knowing:

Dir hat man wohl ins Gehirn geschissen und vergessen umzurühren.
Are you totally out of your mind? (actually: Someone must have shit into your brain and forgotten to stir it)

Mini-Monologue

Some Everyday Scheiße

1. Also so einen beschissenen Tag wie heute habe ich lange nicht gehabt.
2. Erst wollte mein Scheißauto mal wieder nicht starten.
3. Und als ich zu spät zur Arbeit kam, habe ich von meinem Boss auch noch einen Anschiß bekommen.
4. Dieser Scheißkerl hat mir doch tatsächlich mit der Kündigung gedroht.
5. Was mich betrifft, der Kerl hat bei mir verschissen.

1. I'll tell you, I haven't had a day as shitty as this one in a long time.
2. First this piece of shit I call my car wouldn't start again.
3. And when I got to work late, my boss gave me a hard time.
4. This shithead actually threatened to fire me.
5. As far as I'm concerned, I'm through with that guy.

35

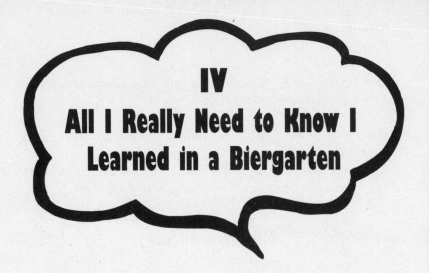

IV
All I Really Need to Know I Learned in a Biergarten

Drinking is an integral part of German culture, and as an avid student of this culture you will probably feel obliged to taste at least a few dozen of the countless brands of beer brewed between the North Sea and the Alps. Beer is Germany's national beverage; you could even say it is to Germans what apple pie is to Americans. Consequently, Germans (men and women alike) spend a considerable amount of their leisure time sitting around in pubs, drinking a good measure of beer, while planning revolutions, tax evasion schemes, or revisions of the national soccer league system. While little skill is required to partake in a discussion on the soccer league—just holler a few names of teams like *"HSV"* or *"F.C. Stuttgart"*—it takes a bit more knowledge to maneuver the world of pubs and bars. You probably already know how to order a beer in German *(Ein Bier bitte!)*, but here are some slang and lingo that will allow you to more fully enjoy this most prominent German pastime—drinking.

Brewskies and Bywords

liquor	**der Alkohol** **der Fusel** (rotgut, cheap liquor; almost bad enough to make you go blind)
beer	**das Bier** **flüssiges Brot** (literally, liquid bread; an expression favored by those who declare that beer is a vital part of their diet) **das Bierchen** (literally, little beer; used by those who like to pretend that one can actually go out and drink just *one* beer; for example, someone might suggest *Komm wir gehen noch ein Bierchen trinken*) **das Pißfix** (literally, piss fast; referring to *Exportbier*, a variety of beer that is supposedly more diuretic than others such as *Pilsener*)
to be thirsty for beer	**einen Bierdurst haben** (another ingenious compound word; literally, to have a beer-thirst)
draft beer	**Bier vom Faß**

SCHEISSE!

stein   **der Krug**
                                     der Humpen
(No, Germans don't actually say stein.)

head *or* froth   **die Blume** (literally, flower)
                                       die Krone (literally, crown)

While Germans are extremely particular about the manner in which their beer is brewed (the over four-hundred-year-old Purity Law that regulates brewing is just about as sacred to Germans as the Constitution is to Americans), they are not above creating some strange and "impure" concoctions with beer. Here are some such mixtures you may encounter:

das Alsterwasser (half beer, half Sprite or Seven-Up; this term is mostly used in Northern Germany)

der Radler (Southern expression for the above)

der Diesel (yes, diesel—a mixture of beer and cola)

die Berlinerweiße (beer with raspberry or woodruff syrup; try it on a hot summer day—it's delicious)

Beer Metaphors

Das ist nicht mein Bier.
That's not my cup of tea.

But also,

Das ist doch nicht mein Bier.
That's none of my business. (as in, Why should I care? Why should I get involved?)

Bei dem sind Hopfen und Malz verloren.
Don't bother with him. He will never change. (literally,
For him hops and malt are lost)

Coolers, Chasers, and Cheers

In some parts of Germany, particularly the wine-growing
regions along the Rhine and the Mosel, beer may actually
take second place to wine. So you may want to give German
wine a try (it's not usually as sweet and sugary as the *Liebfrau-
milch* sold in America).

wine	**der Wein**
	der Schoppen (a glass of wine; for example, when you order a glass of Riesling you would say *Einen Schoppen Riesling bitte.*)
	die Schorle (white wine diluted with soda water)
schnapps	**der Schnaps**
	der Korn (clear schnapps)
	der Klare (same as above)
	ein Kurzer (a glass of schnapps; literally, a short one)
cheers	**Prost!**
	Zum Wohl! (a bit more officious; roughly, to your health)
This one is on me.	**Ich gebe einen aus.**

to drink	**trinken** **saufen** (to drink hard; also refers to the drinking activity of animals) **picheln** (to guzzle) **zechen** (to booze, but can also simply mean "to drink in a pub and run a tab") **zocken** (to booze; also means to play cards)
beverage	**das Getränk** **das Gesöff** (pretty disparaging; you might use this expression if you find the contents of your glass somewhat questionable)
bottle	**die Flasche** **die Pulle** **der Flachmann** (a pint bottle; literally, flat man)

Boozing and Cruising

Just as the roads to drunkenness are numerous, the German language offers a great many words that describe this state:

drunk (adj.)	**betrunken** **besoffen** (stinking drunk) **breit** (smashed; literally, wide) **stramm** (stewed)

	voll (tight; literally, full) **sternhagelvoll** (literally, full of stars and hail; somewhat like soused to the gills) **voll wie'n Eimer** (literally, full as a bucket) **blau** (don't get confused by this one; in German someone who is blue is simply very drunk, not depressed) **duhn** (woozy)
tipsy	**beschwipst einen Schwips haben angesäuselt**
reeking of liquor	**eine Fahne haben** (literally, to have a flag; doesn't need a bag for the breath test)
hangover (noun)	**der Kater** (literally, male cat)
hung over	**verkatert** (for example, *Ich war heute morgen total verkatert*)
to vomit	**sich übergeben** (to throw up) **brechen** (to puke) **kotzen** (to barf) **Bröckchen husten** (literally, to cough up little chunks)
drunkard	**der Alkoholiker der Trinker** (drinker) **der Säufer/die Säuferin** (boozer)

SCHEISSE!

der Saufkopf (boozer)
der Schluckspecht (guzzler, literally, a guzzling woodpecker)

Here's some pure poetry: a slang for moon is *Säufersonne*—drunkard's sun. It takes a drunk genius to come up with this.

bum	**der Penner**
various drinking establishments	**die Kneipe** (pub) **die Bar** **der Biergarten** (Southern outdoor pub) **das Wirtshaus** (tavern) **das Gasthaus** (same as above, except it usually also offers a bed for the night)

drinking tour	**die Picheltour** (serious bar hopping) **die Sauftour** (same as above, just a bit more vulgar) **der Kneipenbummel** (leisurely bar hopping) **die Kneiptour** (a bit of a pun since the word can also refer to a tour of health spas that subscribe to the recipes of the famous Dr. Kneip)
drinking orgy	**das Saufgelage**
drinking buddies	**die Saufkumpanen** **die Saufbrüder**

And since you may not do all your drinking in a pub:

party (noun)	**die Feier** **die Party** **die Cocktailparty** **die Fete** (typical jargon of those under 30)
to celebrate	**feiern** **einen los machen** **die Sau los machen** (literally, to let the sow loose) **Remmidemmi machen** (a high decibel affair)

SCHEISSE!

Mini-Monologue

Let's See How You Fare in a German Pub

1. Ein Bier vom Faß bitte, aber mit 'ner schönen Blume.
2. Was, mußt du schon wieder zum Klo? Hast wohl zuviel Pißfix getrunken.
3. Für meinen Freund hier ein Alsterwasser. Er muß uns nämlich nach unserer Picheltour alle nach Hause fahren.
4. Was ist das denn fur ein Gesöff? Ich hab' doch einen Klaren bestellt.
5. Natürlich weiß ich was ich bestellt habe. Ich bin doch nicht besoffen.
6. Das laß ich mir von dir doch nicht sagen, du alter Saufkopf.

1. A pint of draft, please, but with a nice head.
2. What, you're off to the john again? Guess you drank too much Pißfix.
3. One Alsterwasser for my friend here. He's the one who has to drive us all home after our drinking tour.
4. What kind of poison is that? I ordered a schnapps.
5. Of course I know what I ordered. I'm not stinking drunk.
6. Don't you talk to me like that, you old boozer.

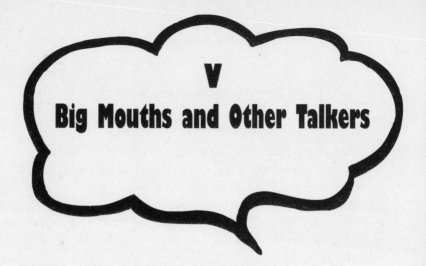

V

Big Mouths and Other Talkers

You may not think of Germans as the most garrulous people in the world, and they probably aren't, but they sure have a lot of words for "talking." Hang around with the natives and you are bound to encounter some of the following:

Babblers . . .

to talk

reden
schnacken (neutral Northern slang for talking)
klönen (to have a chat; Northern)
plauschen (to have a chat; Southwestern)
sabbeln (to gab; to blabber)
quasseln (to chatter)
labern (to talk endlessly and boringly; for example, a student might say *Prof. Müller*

hat mal wieder eine Stunde lang nur gelabert.)
jemanden vollabern (to talk someone's ears off)
faseln (to talk nonsense)
quatschen (depending on context, to talk or to talk nonsense)

to discuss

diskutieren
bekakeln (getting down to the nitty gritty details)
beschnacken (to talk something over, preferably over a beer or two)
palavern (bring your sleeping bag, this may take a while)

a chat

der Klönschnack
der Plausch

talkative

redselig (likes to talk; not necessarily derogatory)
sabbelig (definitely derogatory)
quasselig (ditto)

talker

der Quatschkopf (windbag)
der Sabbelheini (another windbag)
die Quasselstrippe (mostly applies to talkative women)
der Schnacker (talks a lot, but don't believe everything he says)

SCHEISSE!

Another talker/windbag:

Der sagt viel wenn der Tag lang ist.
(literally, He says a lot when the day is long)

Blabbers . . .

braggart (noun)	**der Angeber** **der Prahlhans** (blowhard; will tell everyone who cares to listen about the half dozen women he laid while vacationing on Sylt) **das Großmaul** (big mouth) **der Großkotz** (show-off; only the biggest and best BMW will do for him)
braggart (adjective)	**angeberisch** **großkotzig** (show-offish)
tattletale	**die Petze**
to tattle	**petzen** (*jemanden verpetzen*—to tell on someone)
gossip (subject matter)	**das Geschwätz** **der Klatsch** **der Tratsch**
gossip (person)	**die Klatschtante** (a *yenta*; a woman who makes it her business to know your business and relate it to everyone in the neighborhood)

die **Tratschtasche** (literally, a gossip bag—so you know what she carries around)
die **Tratsche** (short for the above)

And Bamboozlers!

informer

der **Informant**
der **Spitzel** (a term you may hear a lot these days is *Stasispitzel*—someone who informed on his friends and co-workers under the East German regime)

liar

der **Lügner**
der **Spinner** (spins tales)
der **Flunkie** (does a lot of *flunkern*—fibbing)
der **Lügenbaron** (literally, baron of lies; referring to the infamous raconteur Baron Münchhausen)
der **Schwindler** (also, impostor)

lie (noun)

die **Lüge**
das **Seemannsgarn** (yarn; literally, sailor's yarn)
das **Garn** (yarn)
der **Schwindel** (a scheme of lies)

SCHEISSE!

to lie	**lügen** **spinnen** **schwindeln** **Geschichten erzählen** (to tell stories)
sweet talker	**der Süßholzraspler** (literally, someone who is grating licorice, which in its unprocessed form is a sweet root)
flatterer	**der Schmeichler** **der Sülzer** (shameless flatterer; after listening to him you feel like taking a shower to wash off all those sweet and sticky lies; *Sülze* means aspic) **der Schleimscheißer** (another sycophant; literally, someone who shits slime)
to flatter	**schmeicheln** **jemandem Honig um den Mund schmieren** (to butter up; literally, to smear honey around someone's mouth) **jemandem nach dem Mund reden** (to say exactly what someone else wants to hear)

Now that you know a lot of slang about "talk," how about putting an end to all that noise. Imagine it's 3 A.M. and you have finally made it to your hotel after spending eight hours on an airplane next to a screaming *Balg*. You're lucky to have gotten the last room; but, as you quickly discover, a mediocre opera singer occupies the suite next door—and he is convinced that the early morning hours are his most creative ones. If you are beginning to feel the incredible urge to shut him up, here are a few ways of doing it, progressing from the polite to the downright rude:

Seien Sie bitte still. (formal)/**Sei bitte still.** (informal)
Please be quiet.

Ruhe bitte.
Quiet please.

Halt den Mund!
Keep your mouth shut!

Halt die Klappe!
Shut up!

Halt's Maul!
Shut the fuck up!

Mini-Monologue

Keep Talking

1. Du dein Freund ist ein ganz schönes Großmaul. Der erzählt uns den ganzen Abend nur von diesem unterernährten halb blinden Bären den er angeblich in Kanada erlegt hat.
2. Laß uns mal von etwas anderem quatschen. Hast du gehört, daß der Meier auch ein Stasispitzel war?

SCHEISSE!

3. Ja genau, dieser Sabbelheini, das ist der Meier. Als ich ihn das letzte mal gesehen habe, hat er mich über Versicherungsbetrug vollgelabert. Als hätte er davon eine Ahnung.
4. Was ist denn so der neuste Klatsch aus Gimmelshausen? Nicht daß ich 'ne Tratsche bin. . . . Ich bin halt nur neugierig.
5. Was, der alte Lügenbaron spinnt noch immer sein Garn? Ich wunder mich nur, daß ihm noch jemand zuhört.
6. Dieser Süßholzraspler Jensen ist jetzt ein Scheidungsanwalt? Das darf nicht wahr sein. Wann er wohl eine seiner Klientinnen vor den Altar schleppt.
7. Ruf mich morgen mal an, dann klönen wir noch ein bischen.

1. Listen, your friend is a real big mouth. He has spent all evening telling us about this undernourished, half-blind bear he supposedly shot in Canada.
2. Let's talk about something else. Have you heard that Meier was a Stasi informer?
3. Yeah right, the windbag, that's Meier. The last time I saw him he talked my ears off about insurance fraud. As if he knew anything about it.
4. So what's the latest gossip from Gimmelshausen? Not that I'm a gossip . . . I'm just curious.
5. What, that old baron of lies is still spinning his yarn? I'm just surprised that anyone still bothers to listen.
6. That sweet talker Jensen is a divorce lawyer now? I don't believe it. Wonder how long it'll take him before he drags one of his (female) clients off to the altar.
7. Give me a call tomorrow and we'll chat some more.

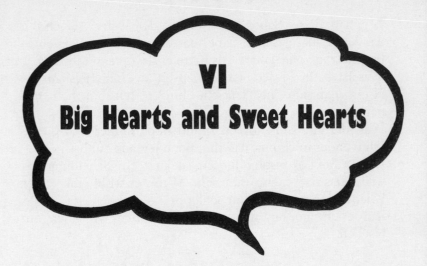

VI
Big Hearts and Sweet Hearts

Of course, not all German slang is downright dirty or disparaging, though the preceding chapters may have given you that impression. In fact, quite a few compliments and heartfelt emotions are best expressed with the aid of colloquialisms and slang.

Friends, Flirts, and Fervor

Der ist in Ordnung.
He's all right. (as in, He's one of us)

Mit ihm könnte man Pferde stehlen.
He's a great guy. You can do anything with him. (literally, You could steal horses with him)

big hearted	**großherzig**
generous	**generös**

SCHEISSE!

großzügig
spendierfreudig (always
ready to buy you a drink)

A bit of *Süßholz*—sweet talk:

Du bist 'ne Wucht.
You're great. (*Wucht* literally means force)

Du bist ein Schatz.
You're a darling. (literally, You're a treasure)

Du bist ein Engel
You are an angel.

Wenn ich Dich nicht hätte ...
If it weren't for you ...

Pledges of Love and Lust

Du bist mein Ein und Alles.
You are everything to me.

Mein süßer Schatz.
My sweet darling/treasure. (literally, treasure)

Mein Schätzchen.
My little darling/treasure.

But also:

Schatz, kannst du mir hiermit mal helfen?
Honey, can you help me with this? (note that *Schatz* is often used as an address like "honey")

Sweet talk bordering on the kinky:

Man to Woman

Meine süße Maus./Mein süßes Mäuschen.
My sweet mouse./My sweet little mouse.

Du süße Biene.
You sweet honey bee.

Mein schnuckeliges Häschen.
My cuddly little rabbit.

Woman to Man

Du toller Hirsch.
You mad, dare-devilish, great deer. (the amazing thing about *toll* is that it can mean all these things)

Du toller Hecht.
You devil of a man. (literally, You mad pike)

Mein toller Hengst.
My great stallion.

Love and Madness

Ich bin verrückt nach dir.
I'm crazy about you.

Du machst mich ganz wild.
You make me crazy (wild).

SCHEISSE!

Ich liebe dich. Du bist der (die) einzige für mich.
I love you. You are the only one for me.

to be in love	**verliebt sein** **verknallt sein** **verschossen sein**

Ich bin in dich verliebt.
I'm in love with you.

Ich habe mich in ihn verknallt.
I have fallen for him.

Ich habe mich in sie verschossen.
I'm head over heels in love with her.

to be heartsick	**Liebeskummer haben**
to adore	**verehren** (can also mean to honor or esteem) **vergöttern** (to turn someone into a god) **anhimmeln** (to look up enraptured at someone; literally, as if he/she were the sky)
to spoil	**verwöhnen** **verhätscheln**
darling	**Liebling** (both in the sense of "favorite" and "loved one") **Schatz** (literally, treasure)
sweetie	**Süßer (m)/Süße (f)**
lover	**Geliebter (m)/Geliebte (f)**

SCHEISSE!

affair   **die Affaire**
das Verhältnis
das Bratkartoffelverhältnis
(literally, home fries affair;
typically, when a man has a
great setup, someone who
cooks and cleans in exchange
for occasional affection)
die Bettgeschichte (literally
translates as bedtime story,
but means "one-night
stand")

Mini-Monologue

Let's See How Smooth Your Sweet Talk Is

1. Mensch, du bist ein Schatz. Wie hast du das nur hingekriegt?
2. Liebling, du bist mein ein und alles. Ich möchte dich mein lebenlang verwöhnen.
3. Mein süßes Mäuschen, du hast keine Ahnung wie sehr ich dich vermisse.
4. Ich bin ganz verrückt nach dir. Wann kann ich dich wiedersehen?
5. So sehr habe ich mich noch nie verknallt.
6. Ich kann nicht anders, ich vergötter dich vollkommen.

1. You're a treasure. How did you do this?
2. Darling, you're everything to me. I want to spoil you for the rest of my life.

3. My sweet little mouse, you have no idea how much I miss you.
4. I'm crazy about you. When can I see you again?
5. I've never fallen so deeply in love before.
6. I can't help myself. I adore you like a goddess.

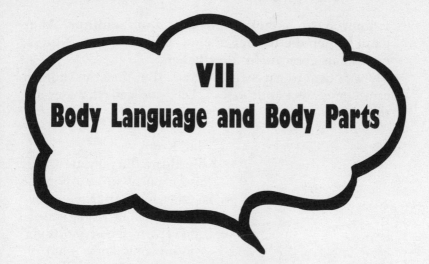

VII
Body Language and Body Parts

No, not gestures (unlike Spaniards or Italians, Germans don't really use a whole lot of expressive body language) but what to call the parts. Of course, you probably already know many of the clinical terms for "hand" and "foot" etc., but really how far can you get with these words? Besides, your well intentioned German teacher probably grossly neglected certain parts of the anatomy. Well, it's time to make up for such omissions. And hopefully real-life experiences will later put your knowledge to the test.

From Top to Bottom

body	**der Körper**
figure	**die Figur**
	die Bombenfigur (great figure; can apply to men and women)

Früher hatte meine Frau eine Bombenfigur. Aber dann kamen die Kinder, meine süßen Kleinen. Nun ja, man kann eben nicht alles haben.
My wife used to have a great figure. But then the children came, my sweet little ones. Well, you can't have everything.

head
> **der Kopf**
> **die Birne** (literally, pear; this also happens to be a popular epithet for Germany's chancellor, Helmut Kohl, and if you've seen pictures of him you probably know why)
> **die Nuß** (bean; literally, nut)

If a horde of skinheads yells at you, **Heh Alter, du kriegst gleich eins auf die Nuß** (Hey, old one, you'll get one over the head), I suggest you try to get away as quickly as possible and save your rage for later. (Perhaps you'll run into one of them when he's by himself sometime.)

face
> **das Gesicht**
> **die Visage** (though it's derived from the French and sounds polite, it basically means "mug")
> **die Fratze** (mug, but can also mean grimace; for example, *Fratzen schneiden* means "to grimace" or "make faces")
> **die Maske** (mask)

There is also the term **Schnute**. While it actually refers to the mouth (literally, snout), you can use it to say "Don't make such a sour face"—*Mach nicht so eine Schnute.*

mouth

der Mund
die Klappe
das Maul (pretty vulgar unless it's referring to an animal's snout)
die Schnauze (ditto)
die Fresse (also pretty vulgar, though the word merely implies that we use our mouths to make pigs of ourselves)

Again, if your friendly neighborhood skinhead tells you, **Halt's Maul oder ich polier dir die Fresse** (literally, Shut up, or I'll polish your trap), you may just be better off to hold your tongue for the time being.

nose

die Nase
der Riecher (literally, smeller)
der Rüssel (nozzle)
die Rotznase (snot nose; can also mean "a snotty nosed little kid")

Dafür habe ich einen Riecher.
I've got a nose for that.

Der hat seine Nase aber auch überall drin.
He's got his nose in everything. (i.e., he is nosy)

Ich habe die Nase voll von dir.
I've had it up to here with you. (literally, I've got my nose full of you)

ears

die Ohren
die Löffel (literally, spoons)
die Elefantenohren (I guess it's self-evident what size they are)
die Segelohren (literally, sail-ears—I mean, why use a spinnaker when you have a set of ears like these)

Oddly, quite a few sayings in German involve ears. Here are just a couple:

Er hat was hinter den Ohren.
He is smart./He has brains. (literally, He's got something behind his ears)

But,

Du kriegst gleich was an die Ohren.
I'm going to slap you in the face. (literally, You'll get something on your ears)

Also,

die Ohrfeige means "the slap in the face."

Er liegt mir schon seit Tagen mit dieser Sache auf den Ohren.
He's been nagging me about this thing for days. (literally, He's been lying on my ears with this thing for days)

SCHEISSE!

Ich hau mich aufs Ohr.
I'll go to sleep. (literally, I'll beat myself on the ear—try to understand that one)

eyes

die Augen
die Gucker (peepers; the verb *gucken* means "to look" or "to peep")
die Glotzaugen (pop eyes)
blaues Auge (black eye)

In moments of exasperation:

Hast du keine Augen im Kopf?
Are you blind? (literally, Don't you have eyes in your head?)

hand

die Hand
die Flosse (fin)
die Pfote (small paw; a way of saying "Hands off!" would be *Pfoten weg!*)
die Pranke (big paw; imagine Frankenstein's dainty creature)
die Grabsche (literally, grabber; a greedy hand or one that makes unwelcomed advances)

foot

der Fuß/die Füße (feet)
die Flosse (fin; can refer to hand or foot)
der Treter (literally, kicker)

buttocks	**das Gesäß** (quite literally, what you sit on) **der Hintern** (behind; back-side) **das Sitzfleisch** (literally, seat-flesh) **der Popo/der Po** (tush) **der Arsch** (ass)

Note, **Sie hat kein Sitzfleisch**, does not mean "She doesn't have an ass" but "She can't sit still for very long."

Apropos *Arsch*, here are a few usages of this earthy word:

Mir ging der Arsch auf Grundeis.
I was scared shitless. (literally, My ass went on ice)

am Arsch der Welt
(literally, at the ass of the world—meaning "far off from any interesting place")

den Arsch zukneifen
to kick the bucket (pretty vulgar; literally, to close one's ass tight)

belly	**der Bauch** **der Bierbauch** (beer belly) **die Wampe** (gut) **der Rettungsring** (literally, life preserver) **der Ersatzreifen** (spare tire)
breasts	**die Brüste** **der Busen** (bust) **die Titten** (tits)

SCHEISSE!

der **Vorbau** (something akin
to a front porch)
die **Möpse** (literally, lapdogs)
dicke Dinger (pretty lewd;
literally, fat things)
die **Ohren** (yes, ears, and
you'll see why)

A woman with a **Vorbau** is basically top heavy and may
have a hard time looking at her toes. However, if she's not
simply fat but well endowed, she may elicit the following
comments: **Mensch, die Braut hat pralle Möpse!** (Man,
that chick has a bursting pair of lapdogs!) or **Guck dir die
dicken Dinger an. Da möchte man doch ein Knopf an**

ihrer Bluse sein. (Look at those big bazongas. I wouldn't mind being a button on her blouse.)

Now, you may wonder how ears fit into this. Imagine the following scenario: a couple of guys are hanging out in the pub and a woman with big bouncy breasts passes their table. But what can they say these days and not get themselves into trouble? Well, **Guck. Hat die nicht schöne Ohren?** (Look. Doesn't she have beautiful ears?). Even if the woman figures out that it's not at all her ears they are admiring, the comment is so innocuous sounding, it's hard to get worked up about it. Besides, if their words are accompanied by sweet smiles, she may even enjoy the compliment.

One last word on this subject matter. If a woman has little to show for in terms of a *Vorbau*, you may hear someone call her a **BMW**, that is a **Brett mit Warzen** (board with warts). So you see, a BMW isn't always such a hot item.

Odds and Ends

nipples	**die Brustwarzen** (literally means "breast warts"; proper, but a pretty ugly sounding word; whoever came up with this word must not have enjoyed them very much)
	die Kirschen (literally, cherries)

Finally, the most vital parts—the family jewels. While it's good to know the proper terms (and if you don't already know them, you will learn them here), the profane ones certainly offer more to the imagination.

penis

der Penis
der Schwanz (literally, tail)
der Pimmel (derived from the word for pestle—as in, pestle and mortar; makes sense to me)
der Lümmel (literally, oaf or lout)
die Latte (log, bone; literally a board—imagine a two-by-four)
die Morgenlatte (morning log)
der Strullermann (*strullen* is slang for urinating)

testicles

die Hoden
der Sack (literally, bag)
die Eier (balls; literally, eggs)

vagina/vulva

die Scheide (proper; like the Latin *vagina*, the word also means "sheath," as in the sheath of a sword)
die Muschi (pussy; as in English, this word can also refer to a pussy cat; amazing how much we think alike)
die Möse (cunt; no one seems to know how this word came about, but be aware that it is pretty vulgar)
die Fotze (cunt or futz; ditto with regard to vulgarity)

And while we're at it, why not learn some slang for those bodily functions rarely mentioned in a textbook; after all, the title of this book alludes to them.

to piss	**pissen**
to pee	**pinkeln**
to tinkle	**strullen**

More elaborate expressions for taking a leak:

eine Stange Wasser in die Ecke stellen
(literally, to put a stick of water in the corner; how one does this is a mystery to me, but that's probably beside the point)

für kleine Bengaltiger gehen/für kleine Uralbären gehen
(translations of these two expressions may make little sense—to go for small Bengali tigers/to go for small Uralian bears—but basically both mean "to go to take a leak")

It should be noted that these baroque expressions for urinating are solely used by men. They seem to take greater pleasure and pride in such abilities than women. And who can blame them—after all, they don't have to crouch but can stand tall and piss in an arch.

to shit	**scheißen**
to crap	**kacken**

Again, the more baroque versions:

für große Bengaltiger gehen/für große Uralbären

SCHEISSE!

gehen
(the significant difference to the above is the adjective
groß—big)

Mini-Monologue

Let's See How You Do with This Able-bodied Slang

1. Sag mal was haben wir denn gestern Nacht so getrieben? Meine Birne dröhnt immer noch.
2. Was, du kannst dich an nichts erinnern? Hast du einen auf die Nuß gekriegt?
3. Ne, aber ich habe zuviel gesoffen. Es ist schon Schwerstarbeit sich so einen Bierbauch wie meinen zu erhalten.
4. Bierbauch? Daß ich nicht lache. Das ist ein Ersatzreifen den du da hast.
5. Apropos, hast du die Alte vom Werner gesehen? Die hat eine Bombenfigur.
6. Und ob ich die gesehen habe. Wer kann denn solche dicken Dinger übersehen?
7. Einen knackigen Arsch hat sie auch.
8. Ich komm gleich wieder. Ich geh nur mal eben für kleine Uralbären.

1. Say, what the hell were we doing last night? My head is still ringing.
2. What, you can't remember a thing? Did someone hit you over the bean?
3. No, but I drank too much. It's hard work to maintain a beer belly like mine.
4. Beer belly? My ass. That's a spare tire you got there.

5. By the way, did you see Werner's wife? She's a bombshell.
6. Of course I saw her. Who could overlook those heavy hooters?
7. She's got a well-shaped ass, too.
8. I'll be back in a second. I'm just gonna go take a leak.

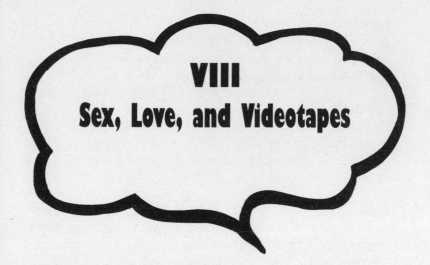

VIII
Sex, Love, and Videotapes

Consider the end of the previous chapter a prelude—
Vorspiel or foreplay. You learned a lot of new terms, and
now it's time to place them in their context—sex. The German language is not unlike English in that the proper terms
for sex are often very clinical, but thank God we have slang
for comic and romantic relief.

Just Do It

Various slangs and euphemisms for "having sex":

Sex haben
to have sex

miteinander schlafen
to sleep with one another

mit jemandem ins Bett gehen
to go to bed with someone

bumsen

to fuck (probably the most common vulgarism for "having sex"; has become almost acceptable—nonetheless, watch out in whose company you're using it)

vögeln

to fuck (literally, mating like birds; a fairly popular word with a long history—first used in medieval times; probably what the duke said to the duchess when he felt raunchy)

ficken

to fuck (originally meant simply "to move back and forth" or "to rub," but nobody is using it in that sense anymore; clearly, you can see the relation to "fuck")

rammeln
to hump (*rammeln* is derived from *Rammler*—male hare)

Sport of Venus

Some more vital *Vulgaritäten:*

blasen
to blow

kommen
to come

einen hoch kriegen
to get it up

ein Rohr kriegen
to get a hard-on (literally, to get a pipe)

wichsen
to jack off (note that *Wichser*, the noun derived from the
above, is a pretty strong epithet)

eine schnelle Nummer
a quicky (literally, a fast number)

die Hobbyflecken
(slang for semen stains)

**Nach der schnellen Nummer in den Büschen, konnte
man deutlich die Hobbyflecken auf seiner Hose sehen.**
After the quicky in the bushes, you could clearly see the
semen stains on his pants.

"In the Beginning . . ."

How it all gets started:

sexy	**sexy** (has been borrowed for so long, Germans no longer think of it as an English word)
	Sex-Appeal haben (obviously, to have sex appeal; see what happens when English expressions become germanized)
erotic	**erotisch** **sinnlich**
horny	**geil** **spitz** **lüstern** (lascivious, lecherous)
old lecher	**alter Lüstling** **alter Lustmolch** (literally, lusty old salamander) **der alte Grabbelheini** (can't keep his hands to himself)
virgin	**die Jungfrau** (as in, *Ich bin doch noch Jungfrau!*—But I'm still a virgin!)
to have the hots for someone	**auf jemanden scharf sein**
seductive	**verführerisch**

76

to seduce

verführen
betören (to bewitch; to beguile)

seductress

die Verführerin
die Anmachfrau (definitely no *Jungfrau*)

to be rigged up

aufgetakelt sein (also shares the same nautical meaning)
aufgedonnert sein (implies a rainbow display of makeup)

to hit on someone

jemanden anmachen (can also mean "to try to pick a fight with someone")

DIE ANMACHFRAU

DER ALTE LUSTMOLCH ←

jemanden anmeiern
jemanden anbaggern (not a
very subtle maneuver; a *Bag-*
ger is an excavator)

Merkst du gar nicht, die wollte dich anmachen?
Don't you realize, she was trying to hit on you?

Hast du etwa meine Freundin angemeiert?
Were you trying to hit on my girlfriend?

to pick up (women/men)   **aufreißen** (a pretty graphic
word; literally, to rip open)

Sag mal, wo kann man denn hier mal ein paar Mädels
aufreißen?
Say, where is a good place around here to pick up some
girls?

to flirt   **flirten**
anbandeln (more serious;
this flirt may actually lead
somewhere)

to kiss   **küssen**
knutschen/rumknutschen
(a bit derogatory; what someone who is jealously watch-
ing would say)

to neck   **schmusen**

bra   **der BH** (short for
Büstenhalter)

lingerie	**die Reizwäsche** (*reizen* means "to stimulate or excite")

A few useful snippets:

Das läßt mich kalt.
That doesn't interest me./That doesn't turn me on. (literally, That leaves me cold)

Du machst mich ganz heiß.
You turn me on. (literally, You make me hot)

Du törnst mich echt an.
You really turn me on. (*antörnen* is mostly a Northern term)

Ich halt's nicht mehr aus.
I can't take it any longer.

Gehen wir zu dir oder zu mir?
Are we going to your place or mine?

The Episcene

Strangely, there are many slang words for male homosexuals but few for female ones. You may want to use some of the following words with caution since they are usually perceived as insults (it all depends on who is talking to whom).

gay man	**der Schwule/ein Schwuler** (used to be an insult but has become pretty acceptable)

gay (adj.)	**schwul** **gay** (some Germans are beginning to use the English word)
faggot	**die Schwuchtel** (implies more femininity; more like a queen) **der Homo**
drag queen	**die Tunte** (*Tuntenball* refers to a gathering and competition of drag queens)

Some more roundabout expressions:

ein warmer Bruder
(literally, a warm brother)

Er ist anders rum.
He's the other way.

Er ist vom andern Stern./Er ist vom andern Ufer.
(literally, He's from another planet./He's from the other shore.)

lesbian	**die Lesbierin** **die Lesbe** (lesbo)

Hostesses and Other Hustlers

Of course, since prostitution is legal in Germany and many of the major cities have thriving red-light districts, you may quite innocently (or less so) stumble upon "women of ill repute." In any case, you wouldn't want to be unprepared, so here is some useful lingo for your nocturnal excursions.

Na Kleiner, komm doch mal rüber.
Hey sweetie (little one), why don't you come over here. (a likely solicitation if you walk down a whore-lined street)

prostitution	**die Prostitution**
	das horizontale Gewerbe
	(literally, the horizontal business)
prostitute (female)	**die Prostituierte**
	die Hure (whore)
	die Nutte (hooker)
	die Edelnutte (*edel* means "noble," or "high grade," so this is not a whore of the streetwalking variety, but one with an answering service; just one piece of advice, don't call her *Edelnutte* to her face)
	das Callgirl (just a fancier word for *Edelnutte*)
	die Hostesse (they sometimes advertise their services under this title in newspapers; you see how confusing it can get for Germans when the manager of an American restaurant asks them if the hostess has been taking care of them)

	die Streekdeern (Low German—i.e., Northern dialect for streetwalker; in case you have ever wondered what a St. Pauli Girl really is, she is a *Streekdeern;* St. Pauli is the main red-light district of Hamburg and probably the largest one in Germany) **die Dominatrix** (if you are into bondage, she'll tie you up and more)
prostitute (male)	**der Stricher/Strichjunge** (usually referring to boys)
to walk the streets	**auf den Strich gehen** (literally, to walk the line) **anschaffen gehen** **anschaffen** (literally, to procure)
pimp	**der Zuhälter**
prostitute's customer	**der Freier** (a pretty delusionary view of the matter; literally means "suitor")
whorehouse	**das Hurenhaus** (literally, whorehouse, but not as commonly used as the two below) **das Bordell** (brothel) **der Puff**
brothel keeper	**die Puffmutter**

striptease bar

das Stripteaselokal
die Stripteasestube (used
jokingly, referring to a small
version of the above; *Stube*
means "room," especially
"living room")

Safe Haven

But in the midst of all the excitement, don't forget your
Verhüterli.

condom

das Kondom
der Präser (rubber; short for
Präservativ—prophylactic)
das Verhüterli (short for
Verhütungsmittel—
contraceptive device; the
Swiss diminutive *-li* is added
simply for the sake of
humor—German speakers
north of the Alps invariably
find the sound of Swiss German very entertaining)
der Pariser (French letter)
die Lümmeltüte (raincoat;
though literally, oaf bag)
die Güllehülle (literally,
manure wrapper—plays on
phonetic similarity to sounds
in the Turkish language)

Mini-Monologue

Sharpen Your Skills and Quicken Your Tongue

1. Hat dir heut schon mal jemand gesagt wie schön du bist? Nein? Habe ich dir schon gesagt, daß ich dich bumsen möchte?
2. Sag mal, deine Anmache ist ja nicht gerade sehr subtil. Aber das gefällt mir.
3. Gestern saß ein junges Pärchen neben mir in der U-Bahn, die haben so rumgeknutscht, ich dachte sie würden da und dort anfangen zu vögeln.
4. Es war etwas komisch da so zu sitzen, aber ich muß zugeben, angetörnt hat mich das schon.
5. Die Nutten in meiner Straße hingegen lassen mich ganz kalt. Das sind alles nur aufgedonnerte Fregatten.
6. Dieser alte Grabbelheini hat schon wieder versucht mir unter den Rock zu fassen.
7. Verdammte Scheiße! Jetzt ist mir der Präser geplatzt.

1. Has anyone told you today how beautiful you are? No? Have I told you that I want to fuck you?
2. You know, your pickup line is not exactly very subtle. But I like it.
3. Yesterday, a young couple was sitting next to me in the subway. The way they were making out, I thought they would start fucking right then and there.
4. It was a bit awkward sitting next to them, but I have to admit that it turned me on.

5. On the other hand, the hookers on my street don't turn me on at all. They are all just dressed up old hags.
6. Can you believe it, that old letch was trying to get his hand under my skirt again.
7. Goddamn it! Now my rubber burst.

IX
Made in Germany
(or Germans at Work)

What's behind that German *Wirtschaftswunder*? Germans have a reputation for being hardworking people—they produce wonderful cars, cameras, and liverwurst—but just how industrious are they? Considering that the average person works only 37.5 hours a week, and that a worker enjoys four to six weeks of paid vacation (now, don't turn green), Germans are either extraordinarily hardworking or this notion of a German work ethic is an old myth. But whether they actually are hardworking or not, Germans sure like to complain about work. And, of course, like everyone else, they like to complain about their bosses and gossip about co-workers. So if you are planning on taking a job in Germany or simply hanging out with some real-life hardworking Germans, you'll now learn how to join in on this ritual of complaining. For example, words like **schuften** and **ackern** are perfect for a tirade on how you have been exploited or underappreciated.

SCHEISSE!

Labor, Leaders, and Lamentations

to work

arbeiten
schuften (implies hard labor; watch out, the noun *Schuft* does not refer to a hardworking person, but a scoundrel)
ackern (also, implies hard labor; literally, refers to plowing a field)
schaffen (fairly neutral; commonly used in Southwest Germany; but watch out, a small prefix can turn it into *anschaffen*—see page 82 on prostitutes)
malochen (again, implies hard labor; mostly used in the heavily industrialized *Ruhrgebiet*; originates from the Yiddish *melocho*)

So if you feel like complaining about how hard you've been working, you might want to say:

Ich habe geschuftet wie noch nie.
I've been working my ass off.

Or if you are not too enthusiastic about facing yet another Monday, you might say:

Am Montag muß ich wieder malochen.
On Monday I'll have to sweat and slave again.

to twiddle (your) thumbs · **Däumchen drehen**

Abwarten und Tee trinken.
Let's wait and see. (basically, Wait and drink tea)

Big Shots and Would-be Bosses

boss · **der Chef/die Chefin**
der Boss (there is no feminine version of this noun; however, you can say *Sie ist der Boss*—she is the boss)
der Häuptling (honcho; literally, chief)
der Oberhäuptling (head honcho)
der Mufti (someone who likes to play the boss; literally, a mufti—an Islamic legal scholar)
der Obermufti (same as above only even more exaggerated)
der Big Mäc (McDonald's has invaded the German language!; akin to a big weenie)
kleiner Napoleon (fat little balding man who is playing the boss)

top executive · **der/die leitende Angestellte**
das große Tier (big gun; literally, big animal)

SCHEISSE!

Down the Ladder

secretary   **die Sekretärin/der Sekretär
die Tippse** (not taken too
kindly even though it literally translates into "typist"; if
you have learned that secre-
taries are often more power-
ful than their bosses, you'll
know better than to call a
secretary *Tippse* to her face)

brownnoser	**der Arschkriecher** (*Arsch*=ass, *Kriecher*=crawler; get the meaning?)
yes-man	**der Jasager**
complainer	**der Nörgler** **der Meckerheini**
to complain	**nörgeln** **meckern**
to be pissed off	**sauer sein**
to cut someone down	**jemanden zusammen-stauchen**
know-it-all	**der Besserwisser** **der Klugscheißer** (literally, someone who shits wisdom)

A new variation of *Besserwisser* is **Besserwessi**—**Wessi** being the slang for "West German." In fact, many **Ossis** (East Germans) feel that their towns and cities are being invaded by hordes of *Besserwessis* who are imparting their wisdom about every aspect of life, from how to run a government to how to fold your toilet paper when you're wiping your ass. From what I've seen, I can't blame the *Ossis*.

stickler	**der Rosinenscheißer** (literally, someone who shits raisins) **der Korinthenkacker** (oh, these subtle differences: someone who craps currants)
to be a stickler	**kleinkariert sein** (*kariert* means "plaid")

SCHEISSE!

bureaucrat	**der Bürokrat** **der Tintenpisser** (literally, ink-pisser)
gofer	**der Laufbursche** **das Mädchen für alles** (literally, the girl for everything; while it may sound quite suggestive, the term is sometimes used as a compliment, meaning that someone is capable of doing many different jobs)
good-for-nothing	**der Nichtsnutz** **der Taugenichts**
loser	**der Versager** **die Niete** **die Null**
wimp	**die Flasche** (literally, bottle) **der Waschlappen** (literally, washcloth)
lazy bunch	**faules Pack**
to call in sick	**sich krank melden** **krankfeiern** (literally, to celebrate illness) **blau machen** (calling in with a cold, but driving to the beach)

If one is to believe German economists, the German federal deficit could be reduced greatly if Germans cut down on their favorite celebration—*Krankfeiern*.

the end of the work day   **der Feierabend**

Komm laß uns Feierabend machen.
Let's call it a day.

after-work drink (beer)   **das Feierabendbierchen**

Money Matters

You've already learned various slangs for money, but what about making some?

den großen Reibach machen
to make a killing (literally, to make great profits; *Reibach* is derived from the Yiddish *rewach*—profit or interest)

sich dick und dämlich verdienen
(something along the lines of "to earn so much that you're becoming fat and stupid"; obviously there is a note of disgust or envy in this expression)

On the other hand, if you think people grossly overestimate your wealth:

Ich bin doch nicht Krösus!
I'm not Croesus! (*Croesus* was a 6th century B.C. king of enormous wealth.)

Ich bin doch nicht Rockefeller!
I'm not a Rockefeller!

Denkst du ich bin ein Dukatenkacker?
Do you think I shit money?

Spongers and Dusters

Less admirable and shady ways of making a living:

schnorren/der Schnorrer
to sponge/the sponger

The guy who is a habitual smoker but never buys his own cigarettes is definitively a *Schnorrer.*

abstauben/der Abstauber
(literally, to dust off and the duster)

Abstauben is a fine art and depends on being at the right place at the right time. The guy who goes over to his buddy's house to see how he is getting on after the terrible accident that cost him his leg becomes an *Abstauber* when he pops the question, "Now that you only got one leg, can I have your bicycle?"

absahnen/der Absahner
to clean up/"the cleaner" (literally, to take off the cream)

The *Absahner* has a supreme understanding of the dynamics of capitalism and knows how to get others to make the hay he's raking in.

con man	**der Hochstapler**
crook	**der Gauner**
	der Ganove

Somehow this list wouldn't seem complete without this old cold-war epithet:

das Kapitalistenschwein
the capitalist pig (Yes, the expression is alive and well in Germany and will probably remain quite viable, considering the *Ossis*' increasing disenchantment with capitalism.)

Insults of the Trade

If you really want to insult a worker, no matter whether blue-collar or white, just tell him or her:

Sie arbeiten ja wie ein Beamter.
You're working just like a civil servant. (the implication is one of being slow, inefficient, and inflexible)

DAS KAPITALISTENSCHWEIN

SCHEISSE!

As benign as this expression may sound, any self-respecting administrator or mechanic will take great offense. German civil servants are renowned for their perpetual don't-bother-me-I'm-on-my-coffee-break attitude. (May God spare you from having any dealings with them!)

Or, if you think your plumber did a shitty job fixing your toilet, or the pages of this book are beginning to fall out after the first reading, and you feel like yelling at someone, try:

Was ist denn das für ein Pfusch!
What kind of shitty piece of work(manship) is this! (the verb *pfuschen* means "to do a quick but lousy job")

Plaudits and Praise

On the other hand, if you want to praise someone for a job well done:

Das ist ja erste Sahne!
That's first class! (literally, first cream)

But since many Germans, especially Northerners, prefer understatements to outright expressions of enthusiasm, try these well-disguised praises:

Gar nicht übel.
Not at all bad.

or

Da kann man nicht meckern.
I can't find anything to complain about. (hard to believe, but in the North this is pretty high praise)

Mini-Monologue

How's Your Working Knowledge
of German?

1. Der Typ mit der Sonnenbrille ist der Oberhäuptling hier. Paß auf, daß du ihn nicht sauer machst.
2. Und der da drüben ist ein richtiger kleiner Napoleon. Ich kann ihn nicht ausstehen.
3. Gestern habe den ganzen Tag für unser Projekt geschuftet und da kommt dieser Kerl doch an und sagt, "Diese Zeichnungen sind ja totaler Pfusch."
4. Der hat es auf mich abgesehen, weil ich es im lezten Jahr fertig gekriegt habe, 20 Tage krankzufeiern. Dieses Jahr werde ich versuchen es auf 30 Tage zu bringen.
5. Habe ich dir schon erzählt, mein Freund hat an der Frankfurter Börse den großen Reibach gemacht und nun weiß er nicht wohin mit dem Zaster? Könnte mir nicht passieren.
6. Paß blos auf, dieser Großhändler ist ein absoluter Gauner. Der wird garantiert versuchen dich anzuscheißen.
7. Die Leute die für ihn arbeiten sind ein faules Pack. Denk blos nicht, daß die auch nur einen Finger für dich rühren werden, wenn du erstmal deine Rechnung bezahlt hast.

1. The guy with the sunglasses is the head honcho here. Make sure you don't piss him off.
2. And that one over there is a genuine little Napoleon. I can't stand him.
3. Yesterday I spent all day slaving for our project, and this guy comes over and says, "These drawings are absolutely lousy."

4. I think he has it in for me because I managed to celebrate twenty days of illness last year. I'm aiming for thirty days this year.

5. Did I tell you my friend made a ton of money at the Frankfurt stock exchange, and now he doesn't know what to do with all the dough? Couldn't happen to me.

6. Watch out, this wholesaler is a complete crook. I guarantee you, he'll try to screw you.

7. The people who are working for him are a lazy bunch. Don't expect them to lift a finger for you once you've paid your bill.

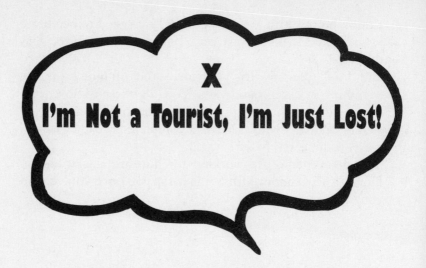

X

I'm Not a Tourist, I'm Just Lost!

Okay, so now you know enough genuine German slang to pass as a native, but once in a while you may still find yourself in a situation when you wish you remembered some of those simple phrases tourists depend on. So let's refresh your memory and add more flavor to the old textbook German.

All Manner of Ways

take a left	**biegen Sie links ab**
take a right	**biegen Sie rechts ab**
straight ahead	**geradeaus**
keep on going straight ahead	**immer geradeaus** **immer der Nase lang** (literally, keep on going where your nose is pointing)
around the corner	**um die Ecke**

SCHEISSE!

But watch out, **jemanden um die Ecke bringen** can also mean "to kill someone," so don't take up just anyone's offer to take you around the corner.

Where is . . . ?	**Wo ist . . . ?**
How far is it to . . . ?	**Wie weit ist es zu . . . ?**
Excuse me. How do I get to . . . ?	**Entschuldigung. Wie komme ich zu . . . ?**
Oh, shit! We're totally lost.	**Ach du Scheiße! Wir haben uns total verlaufen.** (by foot)
	Ach du Scheiße! Wir haben uns total verfahren. (by car, bike, etc.)

Der Zug ist abgefahren.
The train has just left the station.
(also used metaphorically meaning "It's too late for that")

Jetzt sitzen wir in diesem verdammten Kaff fest!
Now we're stuck in this godforsaken place!

Können Sie uns mitnehmen?
Can you give us a ride?

Sie sind unsere einzige Hoffnung.
You are our only hope.

Wo ist die nächste Kneipe?
Where is the nearest pub?

Akzeptieren Sie Kreditkarten?
Do you accept credit cards?

Wo kann ich Geld umtauschen?
Where can I exchange money?

So'n Schiet! Ich hab' meinen Pass verloren.
Oh, shoot! I lost my passport.

Nein wirklich, ich bin Amerikaner(in).
No, really, I'm an American.

So glauben Sie mir doch!
Please believe me!

police station	**die Polizeiwache**
thief	**der Dieb**
Someone stole my wallet.	**Jemand hat meine Brieftasche geklaut.**

hotel

das Hotel
das Gasthaus (a rural affair)
die Pension (smaller and
less luxurious than a hotel,
but cheaper and often more
personable)

Ich muß mich ausruhen.
I need to get some rest.

Ich habe Blasen an den Füßen.
I have blisters on my feet.

Die tun höllisch weh.
They hurt like hell.

Haben Sie ein Pflaster?
Do you have a Band-Aid?

Fast Food, Food Phrases, and Other Fare

Wo kann ich denn hier etwas zu essen bekommen?
Where around here can I get something to eat?

fast-food stand

der Imbiss (a small booth or
stand where you can get sau-
sages and fries; every enter-
prising East German seems
to have opened one after the
Wall came down)

hamburger

der Hamburger (not to be
confused with the citizens of
the Hanseatic city of Hamburg)

	die Frickadelle (just the patty; often served cold) die Boulette (ditto)
roasted chicken	das Brathähnchen der Broiler (only in East Germany) der Gummiadler (literally, rubber eagle)
sausage	die Wurst (there are too many kinds of sausages to mention them all, but try a Knackwurst or Knacker with hot mustard sometime)

Wurst is so quintessentially German that it has worked its way into many sayings and expressions. Here are just a few involving this piece of meat-filled gut:

Du armes Würstchen.
You poor little thing.

Es geht um die Wurst.
It's a matter of all or nothing. (As you can see, when the stakes get high Germans reach for their favorite phallic symbol.)

Das ist mir Wurst.
I don't give a flying fig./I don't care. (literally, That's sausage to me)

Ich verstehe nur Wurstsalat.
I don't understand a thing you are saying. (literally, All I hear is sausage salad; another version is *Ich verstehe nur Bahnhof*)

SCHEISSE!

restaurant

das Restaurant
das Lokal
das Gasthaus (rural; last
strongholds of authentic
German cuisine)

Was ist denn das für eine Bedienung hier?
What kind of service is this anyway?

Ich habe keinen großen Hunger.
I'm not very hungry.

eine Kleinigkeit essen
to have a bite to eat

Ich habe einen Mordshunger.
I could eat a horse.

meat

das Fleisch (yes, also means
"flesh"; a German immigrant
might easily make the mis-
take of telling her American
butcher, "Oh, you have such
wonderful flesh!")

vegetables

das Gemüse

appetizer

die Vorspeise

dessert

der Nachtisch
die Nachspeise
das Dessert

Haben Sie auch vegetarische Speisen?
Do you have any vegetarian dishes?

Ein Glass Wasser bitte.
A glass of water, please.

A word of advice. If you ask for water in a restaurant, you will most likely get a glass of seltzer water. So if you really want just plain tap water, ask for **Leitungswasser**. The waiter may still give you a strange look (water isn't served as a matter of course in German restaurants), but at least he'll know what you want.

Was ist denn das für ein Fraß?
What kind of muck is that?

Das ist nicht das was ich bestellt habe.
That's not what I ordered.

Die Rechnung bitte.
The check, please.

Fine Art, Fine Sights, and Fun

art museum   **das Kunstmuseum**

art gallery   **die Kunsthalle**
                          die Galerie

Was dem einen sin Uhl, ist dem andern sin Nachtigall.
Beauty is in the eye of the beholder. (Low German; literally means "What's one man's owl is another man's nightingale")

der Kunstbanause
(something along the line of an art ignoramus—there doesn't seem to be a word for this in English; a severe in-

sult to any would-be connoisseur of the fine arts; an hon-
orary title to those who are fed up with modern art that
invokes the response, "I could have done that"—but who,
of course, didn't do it)

Wann schließen Sie?
When do you close?

sights	**die Sehenswürdigkeiten** (literally, things that are worth seeing—in case you wondered why on earth the word is so long)
map	**die Landkarte** (map of an entire region or country) **der Stadtplan** (map of a city)
nightlife	**das Nachtleben** **die Szene** (more specifically, *die Kneipenszene, die Diskoszene,* etc.)
red-light district	**das Bordellviertel** **das Nuttenviertel**

Hier ist nach Mitternacht tote Hose.
There's nothing going on here after midnight. (literally,
It's like a dead pair of pants here after midnight)

In Hamburg ist nachts immer etwas los.
In Hamburg there's always something going on at night.

Mini-Monologue

Tourist Survival Skills

1. Entschuldigen Sie, ich habe mich verlaufen. Wie komme ich denn zum Hotel Benedikt? Das müßte hier ganz in der Nähe sein.
2. Nein, das ist kein Stundenhotel. Aber danke für das Angebot.
3. Kennen Sie ein gutes Restaurant hier in der Gegend? Eins wo die Kellner nicht allzu muffelig sind.
4. Das ist mir egal wer dort verkehrt, solange das Essen gut ist und die Atmosphäre stimmt. Im Gegenteil, vielleicht ist die Atmosphäre ja sogar besser, gerade weil dort die Nutten ihren Kaffee an der Theke trinken.
5. Danke, das ist sehr nett von ihnen, aber ich finde schon alleine hin. Geradeaus auf der linken Seite. Nicht wahr?

1. Excuse me, I'm lost. Can you tell me how to get to the Hotel Benedikt? It should be close to here.
2. No, it's not one of those rented by the hour. But thanks for the offer.
3. Do you know of a good restaurant in this area? One where the waiters aren't too grumpy.
4. Oh, I don't care who frequents the place, as long as the food is good and the atmosphere is right. On the contrary, perhaps the atmosphere is even better because the hookers are drinking their coffee at the bar.
5. Thanks, that's very nice of you, but I think I'll be able to find it myself. Straight ahead on the left-hand side. Right?

XI
Last Words

I'm beginning to feel a bit *mütterlich* about you, my dear reader, so I wouldn't want you to go out in the German streets without knowing a few more vital expressions and phrases.

Echt?
Really?

Denkste!
Fat chance!/The hell you are!/The hell I am! (depends on the context; literally, That's what you think)

Jain.
(hybrid of **Ja** and **Nein**—"Yes" and "No"; used by the clearly indecisive)

Was ist los?
What's up?

Was gibt's neues?
What's new?

Ist was? (or the Northern variation **Is' was?**)
Something the matter? (as in, Quit staring at me unless you're trying to tell me my fly is open)

Willst du was? (sometimes pronounced as one word—
"**Wissuwas?**")
What are you looking at? (literally, Do you want something?; this is pretty hostile stuff, so choose your answer very carefully, if there is time for words)

Hilfe!
Help!

Ist das klar?
Is that clear?

Klar?/Klaro?
Understood?

Klar wie Kloßbrühe.
Understood completely. (literally, Clear as broth.)

Mach den Mund zu, deine Milchzähne werden sauer.
(literally, Close your mouth, your milk teeth are turning sour; to one who continues to gape and doesn't seem to recover from whatever it was that made him drop his jaw)

Das hat mir gerade noch gefehlt!
That's all I needed! (obviously, on the ironic side)

Lieber arm dran als Arm ab.
(loosely, It's better to be poor than to lose an arm; literally, Better poor off than arm off)

SCHEISSE!

Ich weiß wo der Hase lang läuft.
You can't fool me. I know what's going on. (literally, I know where the hare is running)

Mit ihm ist nicht gut Kirschen essen.
He's a grouch. It's hard to get along with him. (Who would have guessed? literally, He's not a good one to eat cherries with)

Hör auf um den heißen Brei herumzureden.
Stop beating around the bush. (literally, Stop talking around the hot mush)

Komm zur Sache!
Get to the point!

to be lucky	**Glück haben** (literally, to have luck) **Schwein haben** (literally, to have a pig; to Germans, a pig symbolizes good luck—and lots of sausages) **Sott haben** (literally, to have soot; according to folklore, touching a chimney sweep brings luck)

Mensch! Habe ich ein Schwein gehabt.
Man! I was lucky. (*Schwein* and *Sott* are both used if by a stroke of luck you escaped some terrible misfortune)

to be unlucky	**Pech haben** (literally, to have pitch)
unlucky person	**der Pechvogel**

to be afraid	**Angst habe** **Bammel haben** **Schiß haben** (to be chicken, though *Schiß* suggests something else) **Muffensausen haben** (to be scared shitless)

Ich kriegte echt Muffensausen als der zweite Motor ausfiel.
I was scared shitless when the second engine failed.

Finally, it wouldn't hurt to be aware of some regional name calling. You already know that East Germans are called *Ossis* and West Germans are *Wessis*, but there is more to it. Prior to reunification, Germans focused more on the differences between Northerners and Southerners than between capitalist-raised Westerners and socialist-suckled Easterners. And while, for the time being, everyone in the West seems to be preoccupied with Ossi bashing, the old feuds between the North and the South are far from forgotten.

Bavarian (Southerner)	**der Bayer** **der Saubayer** (*Sau* = sow) **"ein kleines diebisches Bergvolk"** (a phrase popularized by a Northern comic strip; literally, a small thieving mountain tribe)
Northerner	**das Nordlicht** (literally, northern light; applied to those living in the coastal regions; I have yet to meet a Northerner who minds this

title, although Bavarians are sure it's an insult)
der Saupreuß (basically means nothing less than "piggish Prussian"; applied to anyone living north of Bavaria, regardless of whether their region had been part of Prussia)
der Fischkopf (literally, fishhead; obviously an expression of envy by those who live too far from the ocean to enjoy good seafood)

East Germany	**Ostdeutschland** **die ehemalige DDR** (the former GDR; the politically correct version) **der Osten** **das Ossiland** **drüben** (over there) **die NFL** (sorry, not the National Football League, but *Neuen Fünf Länder*—New Five States)
West Germany	**Westdeutschland** **der Westen** **das Wessiland** **drüben** (it all depends on your perspective)

Mini-Monologue

Alles Klar?

1. Was ist los? Du siehst so nachdenklich aus. Hast du wieder Schwierigkeiten?
2. Schwierigkeiten? Nö. Ich habe eine ganz super tolle absolut phänomenale Idee.
3. Echt? Na schieß mal los.
4. Ich habe einen Plan wie du und ich im Ossiland ein ganz großes Geschäft machen können.
5. Du und ich als Geschäftspartner? Denkste! Bin ich blöd? Ich weiß doch wie es deinem letzten Geschäftspartner

ergangen ist. Und sowieso, ich investiere drüben nicht. Ist das klar?

6. Klar wie Kloßbrühe. Um ehrlich zu sein, ich hatte von dir auch gar nichts anderes erwartet, du alter Saupreuß.

1. What's up? You look so pensive. Are you in trouble again?
2. Trouble? No. I have a super, great, absolutely phenomenal idea.
3. Really? Go ahead, shoot.
4. I have a plan how you and I can make big bucks in East Germany.
5. You and I as business partners? Fat chance! You think I'm stupid. I know what happened to your last business partner. And besides, I don't invest money over there. Is that clear?
6. Clear as broth. To tell you the truth, I didn't expect anything else from you, you piggish old Prussian.

XII
Big-Time Test!

No, don't sweat it, this won't be anything like the tests *die gute Frau Schultz* used to give you. After all, you are beyond that, and you probably know a whole lot more "real German" now than your high school German teacher ever did. Test yourself in the next few paragraphs, and you may even have some downright dirty fun. Simply read each narrative and try to find out which famous German literary figure is speaking or being described. If you don't get the answers, don't worry, they're in the back. (But no cheating! *Klar?*). In any case, you'll see the slang you've learned in action and be ready to start dishing it out to the natives.

1. Meine Stiefmutter war die fieseste alte Hexe, die ich je gekannt habe. Schon als kleines Kind mußte ich schuften und ackern und für sie den gesammten Haushalt machen. Aber sie war nicht nur fies und faul, sondern auch noch äußerst häßlich. Sie war häßlich wie die Nacht, und da nützte es ihr wenig sich wie eine alte Hure aufzutakeln. Natürlich störte es sie höllisch so ein hübsches junges Mädel wie mich ständig vor ihrer Nase zu haben. Also versuchte sie mich loszuwer-

SCHEISSE!

den in dem sie einen Jäger überredete, mir in den Wald zu folgen und mich dort zu erschießen. Aber den lieben Armleuchter habe ich derartig betört, daß er nicht mehr wußte wohin mit seinem Schwanz. Nun ja, da wußte ich ihm natürlich zu helfen. Später ließ er mich dann auch aus lauter Dankbarkeit laufen. Aber zurück nach Hause gehen konnte ich natürlich nicht. Wenn ich meinem Vater erzählt hätte was seine Alte für mich geplant hatte, hätte der doch blos gesagt, "Mädel, du bist ja total verrückt." Also schloß ich mich sieben Typen, die hinter den sieben Bergen wohnen, an. Die Jungs sind alle etwas klein geraten, aber das störte mich nicht weiter. Wir hatten ein ganz lustiges Leben zusammen. Zuerst dachte ich die wären alle schwul, aber wie sich zum Glück herausstellte war dem nicht so. Es wäre auch alles bestens gewesen, wenn meine Stiefmutter nicht herausgefunden hätte wo ich war. Ja, und wenn dieser blöde Prinz mich nicht "gerettet" hätte. Nun bin ich mit ihm verheiratet, sitze hier in diesem Kaff und langweile mich zu Tode.

2. Oh Gott ich halt's nicht mehr aus. Ich krieg ja schon ein Rohr wenn ich das Mädchen nur ansehe. Sie ist die süßeste kleine Maus die ich je gesehen habe. Wahrscheinlich ist sie auch noch Jungfrau. Aber was rede ich denn? Natürlich ist sie Jungfrau. Sie hat die Titten einer Jungfrau, das kann ich sehen. Daß sie die Muschi einer Jungfrau hat, davon träume ich. Für diese Kindsfrau würde ich meine Seele an den Satan persönlich verkaufen. Verdammt! Wo ist dieser Teufel wenn man ihn braucht? Zur Hölle mit diesem faulen Hund!

The last one may be a bit tough. But here's a hint: you may have seen the movie version by Volker Schlöndorff.

3. Der kleine Junge holte mal wieder seine Blechtrommel aus dem Schrank, lief hinaus auf die Straße und trommelte

wie ein Wilder. Da lehnte sich seine Nachbarin, eine allseits bekannte Tratschtasche, aus ihrem Fenster heraus. Ihre prallen Möpse hingen über dem Fensterbrett und erdrückten schon beinahe ihre Geranien, als sie lauthals schrie, "Du verdammtes Gör! Wenn du nicht gleich ruhig bist, breche ich dir die Arme und deine Trommelstöcke auch." Aber der kleine Junge ließ sich nicht so leicht einschüchtern und trommelte weiter. Bis die alte Schachtel schließlich anfing ihre Geranientöpfe nach dem Jungen zu schmeißen. Leider traf ihn einer dieser Töpfe auf die Nuß und seit dem ist der Junge nicht mehr einen einzigen Zentimeter gewachsen.

Translations

1. My stepmother was the meanest old witch I've ever known. Even when I was a small child I had to sweat and slave and do all the household chores for her. But she was not only mean and lazy, she was also extremely ugly. She was ugly as the night, and it didn't do her much good to get all rigged up like an old whore. Of course, it bothered the hell out of her to have a young and pretty girl like me constantly under her nose. So she tried to get rid of me by persuading a hunter to follow me into the woods and shoot me there. But I beguiled that dear little idiot until he didn't know what to do with his cock. Well, of course, I knew how to help him. Later, he let me go out of sheer gratitude. But going back home wasn't an option. If I had told my father what his old woman had been up to, he would have said, "Girl, you're out of your mind!" So I ended up joining seven guys who lived on the other side of the Seven Mountains. The boys were all a bit on the short side, but I didn't mind. We had quite a bit of fun together. At first I thought they were gay, but luckily that was not at all the case. Everything would have been just grand, if my stepmother hadn't found

out where I was. Yeah, and if this stupid prince hadn't "rescued" me. Now I'm married to him, trapped in this godforsaken place and nearly bored stiff.

2. Oh God I can't take it any longer! I already get a hard-on just looking at the girl. She is the sweetest little thing I've ever seen. Probably still a virgin. What am I saying? Of course she's a virgin. She has the perky tits of a virgin, that I can see. That she has the pussy of a virgin is what I dream of. I'd sell my soul to Satan to have this child–woman. Damn! Where is this devil when you need him? To hell with that lazy dog!

3. The little boy got his tin drum from the closet, ran out into the street, and began to drum like a wild man. Soon, his neighbor, a woman widely known as a gossip, leaned out of her window. Her hooters (*fat little lapdogs*) hung over the windowsill and were about to crush her geraniums, when she yelled, "You damn brat! If you're not quiet right now, I'm going to break your arms, and your drumsticks too." But the little boy wasn't easily bullied and kept on drumming. That is, until the old hag threw her potted geraniums after him. Unfortunately, one of the pots hit him on the bean. Since then the boy hasn't grown an inch.

Answers

1. Snow White (*Snow White*, the Grimm brothers)
2. Dr. Faust (*Faust*, Johann Wolfgang Goethe)
3. Oskar Matzerath (*The Tin Drum*, Günter Grass)

Glossary

For quick reference, here are some of the words and expressions you will find in this book:

ass	**der Arsch**
asshole	**das Arschloch**
Baloney!	**Quatsch!**
bastard	**der Schweinehund**
to barf	**kotzen**
beer belly	**der Bierbauch**
big mouth (braggart)	**das Großmaul**
to blabber	**sabbeln**
to blow (as in blow job)	**blasen**

blowhard	der Prahlhans
bonehead	der Holzkopf
to booze	zechen, zocken, saufen
boozer	der Säufer
boss	der Chef, der Boss, der Häuptling, der Mufti
bozo	der Heini
brat	der Balg, das Gör
breasts	die Brüste, die Titten
brownnoser	der Arschkriecher
buddy	der Kumpel
bum	der Penner
bureaucrat	der Bürokrat, der Tintenpisser
capitalist pig	das Kapitalistenschwein
to chat	klönen
chauvinist	der Chauvi, der Chauvinist
Cheers!	Prost!

SCHEISSE!

cock	der Schwanz, der Pimmel, der Lümmel
cool	klasse, super, prima, spitze toll, geil
condom	das Kondom, der Präser, der Pariser
con man	der Hochstapler
cop	der Bulle, das Rindfleisch (careful, don't say this to a cop)
crap	die Kacke
crazy	verrückt, nicht ganz dicht, bekloppt
crook	der Gauner, der Ganove
cunt	die Möse, die Fotze
Damn!	Verdammt!
darling	Liebling, Schatz
dimwit	der Armleuchter
dough	die Knete
draft beer	das Bier vom Faß

drinking buddies	**die Saufbrüder, die Saufkumpanen**
drinking orgy	**das Saufgelage**
dude	**der Macker**
Fat chance!	**Denkste!**
fatso	**der Fettsack**
For God's sake!	**Um Gottes Willen!**
to fuck	**bumsen, ficken, vögeln**
Fuck off!	**Verpiß Dich!**
Fuck you!	**Du kannst mich mal am Arsch lecken!**
to gab	**sabbeln**
gay (adjective)	**schwul**
Get to the point!	**Komm zur Sache!**
Go to hell!	**Geh zum Teufel!**
God damn it!	**Verdammt noch mal!**
good-for-nothing	**der Nichtsnutz, der Taugenichts**
gut (belly)	**die Wampe**

SCHEISSE!

half-wit	der Trottel
hangover	der Kater
head honcho	der Oberhäuptling
Help!	Hilfe!
to hit on someone	jemanden anmachen/ anmeiern
hooker	die Nutte, die Hure
horny	geil, spitz
hung over	verkatert
idiot	der Idiot, der Dummkopf, der Holzkopf
to jack off	wichsen
the john	das Klo
to kiss	küssen, knutschen
kiss (noun)	der Kuß, das Küsschen
klutz	der Tollpatsch
know-it-all	der Besserwisser
lesbian (adjective)	lesbisch
lingerie	die Reitzwasche

loser	**der Versager, die Niete, die Null**
muck	**der Dreck**
mug	**die Fratze**
nipples	**die Brustwarzen, die Kirschen**
No!	**Nein! Ne! Nö! Na!**
numbskull	**der Dummkopf**
old bag	**die alte Schachtel**
old fart	**der alte Knacker**
old lecher	**der alte Lüstling**
to pee	**pinkeln**
Peeping Tom	**der Spanner**
penis	**der Penis, der Schwanz, der Pimmel**
pimp	**der Zuhälter**
to piss	**pissen**
to be pissed off	**sauer sein**
pussy	**die Muschi**

SCHEISSE!

quicky	**die schnelle Nummer**
Really?	**Echt?**
rotgut	**der Fusel**
shit (noun)	**die Scheiße, der Scheiß**
shithead	**der Scheißkerl**
shitty	**beschissen**
slowpoke	**der Larmarsch**
slut	**die Schlampe**
smashed	**breit**
So what?	**Na und?**
stewed	**stramm**
stickler	**der Rosinenscheißer, der Korinthenkacker**
sweet talker	**der Süßholzraspler**
sweetie	**Süßer/Süße**
Take a hike!	**Mach 'ne Fliege!**
tattletale	**die Petze**
tipsy	**beschwipst**

tush	**der Po, der Popo**
virgin	**die Jungfrau**
What's up?	**Was ist los?**
whore	**die Hure, die Nutte**
whorehouse	**das Hurenhaus, das Bordell, der Puff**
wimp	**die Flasche, der Waschlappen**
windbag	**der Quatschkopf**
yenta (gossip)	**die Klatschtante, die Tratschtasche**
yes-man	**der Jasager**